COSTA R.

TRAVEL GUIDE

2024

The Ultimate Adventure Destination for Nature Lovers

LUZ F. SMITH

Table Of Content

Chapter 7
Travel Itinerary Planner

Conclusion

Introduction to Costa Rica

Why Visit Costa Rica in 2024?

Costa Rica is a paradise for those who enjoy nature, culture, and adventure. **Here are reasons why you should visit this great country in 2024:**

1. Costa Rica has an astounding diversity of life, hosting more than 5% of the world's species. In their natural habitats, you can see wonderful animals including monkeys, sloths, toucans, macaws, hummingbirds, sea turtles, and more.

2. You can unwind and enjoy Costa Rica's lovely, sunny weather, which has two seasons: dry and wet. From December to April is the dry season, while from May to November is the wet season. Throughout the year, the average temperature is around 27° C (81° F).

3. You may learn about Costa Rica's diverse culture, which has been formed by Spanish, African, Indigenous,

and European influences. Learn about Costa Rica's history, art, music, and food, as well as participate in festivals and celebrations such as Independence Day, Christmas, and Easter.

4. You may have fun and adventure in Costa Rica, which has activities for people of all ages and tastes. Surf, snorkel, fish, zip-line, hike, bike, raft, kayak, horseback ride, and more activities are available. You may also visit Arenal Volcano, Manuel Antonio National Park, La Paz Waterfalls, Papagayo Peninsula, Tamarindo Beach, Rio Celeste, Monteverde Cloud Forest, and Corcovado National Park, which are among the top attractions in Costa Rica.

A Brief History of Costa Rica

Costa Rica is a Central American country with a rich and varied past. Costa Rica's early inhabitants were nomadic hunters who arrived some 10,000 years ago. Later, numerous indigenous cultures arose and interacted with other places, such as the Diquis, Chorotega, and Boruca.

Costa Rica was colonized by Spain in the 16th century and became part of the Captaincy General of Guatemala, a New Spanish province. Costa Rica was a poor and isolated country with little economic or political clout. It declared independence from Spain, along with the rest of Central America, in 1821, and became a member of the Federal Republic of Central America in 1823.

Costa Rica declared independence from the federation in 1838. Several civil wars and coups occurred in the 19th and 20th centuries when various factions fought for power and reforms. The most significant struggle was the 1948 Civil War, which ended in the demise of the army and the establishment of a democratic constitution in 1949.

Costa Rica is well-known for its political stability, social advancement, environmental stewardship, and human rights. Its economy is multifaceted, relying on agriculture, tourism, technology, and trade. It has many national parks and wildlife reserves, making it one of the world's most biodiverse countries.

The Culture and People of Costa Rica

The following are some facts about its culture and people:

1.Costa Ricans and Ticas are friendly nicknames derived from their practice of attaching diminutive suffixes to their language.

2. Spanish is the official language of Costa Rica, although additional languages spoken by various populations include English Creole, Bribri, Ngöbe, Cabecar, Buglere, and Maleku.

3. Costa Rica is well-known for being one of the world's happiest and most environmentally friendly countries. It provides free education and healthcare to all of its residents and safeguards nearly a quarter of its territory from development.

4. Costa Rica has a vibrant art scene, with numerous well-known artistic traditions such as colorful oxcart paintings, pre-Columbian stone spheres, and traditional dances. Francisco Amighetti, who painted rural life and landscapes in Costa Rica, is one of its most recognized artists.

5. Costa Rican cuisine is delectable, with indigenous, Spanish, African, and Asian influences. Gallo pinto (rice and beans), Casado (a meal of rice, beans, salad, meat, and plantains), ceviche (raw fish marinated in lime juice), and arroz con leche (rice pudding) are other popular foods.

The Geography and Climate of Costa Rica

Costa Rica borders Nicaragua, Panama, the Caribbean Sea, and the Pacific Ocean. It has a land area of around 51,100 square kilometers, which is comparable to West Virginia's. Costa Rica is divided into four major geographical regions: the Caribbean lowlands, the highlands, the Guanacaste plains, and the south.

With an annual temperature of roughly 27°C (80°F), the Caribbean lowlands are warm and damp. The biodiversity in this region is high, particularly in the tropical rainforests that dominate the landscape. The lowlands are also home to several of the country's aboriginal communities and a big banana export sector. Beaches, coral reefs, and mangrove swamps are just a few of the attractions along the Caribbean coast.

The country's economy, politics, and culture are centered in the highlands, where the majority of the population resides. This region is made up of the Central and Talamanca mountain ranges, as well as the Central Valley, which is home to San Jose, the capital city. At 900 meters (3,000 feet) above sea level, the highlands offer a mild subtropical climate, with an average annual temperature of around 23°C (74°F). The temperature drops with height, reaching about 15°C (59°F) at 1,500 meters (5,000 feet). The highlands receive more rain than the lowlands, with annual rainfall averages between 1,500 and 2,000 millimeters (60 and 75 inches). Arenal, Irazu, Poas, and Turrialba are among the active volcanoes in the highlands.

The Guanacaste lowlands are located in northwest Costa Rica and encompass sections of the provinces of Guanacaste and Puntarenas, as well as the Nicoya Peninsula. The climate in this area is dry tropical, with an annual temperature of roughly 26°C (79°F). The Guanacaste plains have the shortest dry season in Costa Rica, ranging from November to April. This area is vital for farming and livestock, as well as tourism. There are numerous attractions in the Guanacaste plains, including beaches, national parks, and wildlife reserves.

Costa Rica's southern portion has the wettest climate, with an annual rainfall of more than 3,000 millimeters (120 inches). The climate in this region is humid and tropical, with an annual temperature of roughly 25°C (77°F). The Osa Peninsula, in the southern area, is one of the most biologically varied places on the planet. Beaches, rainforests, waterfalls, and rivers are just some of the attractions of the southern region.

Chapter 1

Planning Your Trip

When To Go

If you're thinking of visiting Costa Rica in 2024, you might be wondering what the best time to travel is. The optimum time to go, however, is determined by your unique preferences and interests. **Consider the following factors when deciding when to visit Costa Rica in 2024:**

1. Costa Rica has Two Seasons: Dry and Wet. The wet season lasts from May to November, whereas the dry season lasts from December to April. The dry season is typically the ideal time to visit Costa Rica, as it provides warm and sunny weather, excellent views, and minimal humidity. The dry season, however, is also the most popular time to visit, which means more travelers, more rates, and less availability. The rainy season is less expensive and quieter, but expect rain, muck, and fog. Some areas, such as the Osa Peninsula and the Caribbean coast, have varying weather patterns and may experience sun or rain at various times of year. On [AccuWeather], you can see the weather forecast for many places in Costa Rica.

2. Activities: Costa Rica has a wide range of activities for all types of people, from adrenaline junkies to nature lovers. Ziplining, hiking, surfing, rafting, snorkeling, animal watching, and relaxing on the beach are some of the most popular things to do in Costa Rica. Some activities, however, are more suited to specific seasons or areas than others. For example, if you want to observe humpback whales at Marino Ballena National Park, the best months to visit are July through October or December through March. The dry season is the perfect time to visit Monteverde's cloud forests or observe the Arenal Volcano erupt. Surfing on the Pacific coast is ideal from May to November. The greatest time to go snorkeling or diving on the Caribbean coast is between September and October.

3. Events: Costa Rica has a rich culture and history, which you may learn about by attending one of the many festivals and events held throughout the year. Carnival in Limon (October), Christmas and New Year's Eve celebrations (December-January), Palmares Fiestas (January), Envision Festival (February), Semana Santa (March-April), Juan Santamaria Day (April), Independence Day (September), and Dia de los Muertos (November) are just a few of the most well-known events. These events are a terrific way to experience Costa Rican food, music, dancing, art, and traditions. They may, however, draw more tourists, resulting in higher pricing and traffic bottlenecks.

How To Get There

If you are planning a vacation to Costa Rica from another nation, here are some actions you Should take to make your journey more convenient:

1. Book a flight to Costa Rica: Your flight options and prices may vary depending on where you are flying from. You can compare different routes and airlines by using a flight search engine such as [Skyscanner] or [Kayak]. Costa Rica's major airports include the following:

- **Juan Santamaria International Airport (SJO):** Costa Rica's primary airport, located near San José.

- **Daniel Oduber Quirós International Airport (LIR):** Costa Rica's second largest airport, located near the Pacific coast in the province of Guanacaste.

- **Toba Bolanos International Airport (SYQ):** A tiny airport in San José that mostly serves domestic and charter aircraft.

2. Obtain a visa: Depending on your nationality, you may be required to obtain a visa to enter Costa Rica. The [official website] of the Costa Rican immigration authorities has information on visa requirements. If a visa is required, you must apply at the closest Costa

Rican embassy or consulate, which may be in another nation. Documents such as your passport, flight itinerary, hotel reservation, bank statement, and travel insurance are required. The visa fee is USD 32, and processing time can range between a few days and several weeks.

3. Be aware of health and safety restrictions: Costa Rica has rigorous health and safety standards in place to prevent the spread of COVID-19 and other infections. Before leaving, you must fill out an online [health pass] and provide documentation of a negative PCR test done within 72 hours of your arrival. You must also have current travel insurance that covers COVID-19-related medical expenditures and quarantine fees. More information is available on the [official website] of Costa Rica's tourism board. In addition, you should verify your government's [travel advice] and see your doctor about any immunizations or drugs you may require for your trip.

4. Pack your belongings: Costa Rica has a tropical climate that is warm and humid all year. There are, however, differences based on height, season, and geography. Pack lightweight, layered clothing, as well as a rain jacket, sunscreen, bug repellent, and a hat. You should also bring sturdy shoes for hiking and experiencing the country's natural wonders. Remember to bring your passport, visa, aircraft tickets, health pass, trip insurance, and any other necessary paperwork.

5. Have fun on your trip: Once you arrive in Costa Rica, you will be astounded by the country's diversity and beauty. It has beautiful beaches, volcanoes, jungles, animal reserves, and cultural attractions to visit. You can also sample its delectable cuisine, learn some Spanish, and mingle with its welcoming locals. Costa Rica's most popular destinations include:

- **San José:** Costa Rica's capital and largest city, including museums, art galleries, parks, marketplaces, and a vibrant nightlife.
- **La Fortuna:** A town near Arenal Volcano with hot springs, waterfalls, zip-lining, rafting, and hiking.

- **Monteverde:** A cloud forest reserve teeming with hundreds of bird, plant, and animal species.
- **Tortuguero National Park:** Known for its turtle-breeding beaches and diverse wildlife.
- **Puerto Viejo:** A laid-back Caribbean seaside village where you can go surfing, snorkeling, diving, and party.

Entry Requirements and Visa

However, before you plan your vacation, you should be aware of your country's entry criteria and visa laws.

The good news is that Costa Rica has a highly accommodating and friendly guest policy. Tourists from any country are welcome in Costa Rica, and there are no COVID-19 testing or immunization restrictions for visitors. **You must, however, meet the following requirements:**

1. A valid passport that will not expire within six months of your arrival date is required.

2. You must have a return flight ticket or onward ticket proving your intention to leave the country before your visa or entrance stamp expires, which is normally within 90 days. A pre-purchased bus ticket, airplane ticket, or proof of passage on a cruise liner can all be used as an onward ticket.

3. You must demonstrate economic solvency for the duration of your visit, which varies depending on your place of origin and the length of your stay. In rare situations, an immigration official may request proof of income, bank statements, or credit card information.

4. When entering or leaving Costa Rica, you must fill out a form at the migration post and report any money equal to or higher than US $10,000, or its equivalent in other currencies, cash, or securities. Before completing the immigration procedures, the declaration must be made.

5. If you are traveling from Angola, Benin, Burkina Faso, Cameroon, the Democratic Republic of the Congo, Gabon, Gambia, Guinea, Liberia, Nigeria, Sierra Leone,

Sudan, Bolivia, Venezuela, Brazil, Peru, Colombia, Ecuador, or the Republic of Guyana, you must have a yellow fever vaccination certificate. This condition also applies to travelers who have spent the previous 14 days in China, Hong Kong, Macao, or Taiwan.

6. If you are traveling from China, Hong Kong, Macao, or Taiwan, you must additionally have documentation proving that you are up to date on your COVID-19 immunization.

7. If you complete these standards, you will be given an entry stamp in your passport indicating how many days you are permitted to stay in Costa Rica as a tourist. The maximum time is 90 days, however, it can vary depending on your country of origin and the immigration official's discretion.

8. If you want to stay longer than your visa allows, you must request for a visa extension at the immigration office in San José or any regional office. The extension costs $100, and you must present proof of economic

soundness as well as a valid cause for your request. You can also leave the nation and re-enter with a fresh entry stamp, but this is not advised because it may create suspicion and result in admission denial.

During your vacation, you must observe the country's laws and regulations, as well as the health protocols established by private companies. You will ensure a safe and happy journey if you do so.

Health and Safety

There are some health and safety dangers that visitors should be aware of and plan for. **Here are tips to help you have a safe and enjoyable trip to Costa Rica:**

1. Before you go, check your government's or the World Health Organization's newest travel and health advisories for Costa Rica. Certain infections, such as COVID-19, hepatitis A, hepatitis B, malaria, measles, and rabies, may necessitate vaccination or the use of prophylactic medication. To enter the country, you may need to bring a negative COVID-19 test result or confirmation of immunization. Consult your doctor at least a month

before your travel to ensure you have all of the necessary vaccines or medications.

2. Avoid drinking tap water or ice prepared from tap water when you arrive, particularly in rural regions or near the ocean. The quality of the water varies depending on location and season, and it may be contaminated with bacteria, parasites, or arsenic. Water that has been bottled or filtered is safer and more widely available. Additionally, you should avoid consuming raw or undercooked foods, including shellfish, meat, eggs, and dairy products. Wash your hands with soap and water regularly, or use an alcohol-based hand sanitizer.

3. When traveling in Costa Rica, be mindful of your surroundings and belongings. Pickpocketing, bag snatching, and car theft are all widespread in tourist regions, public transportation, and congested areas. Keep big quantities of cash and valuables in a safe place or locked in your hotel room. Unsolicited assistance from strangers, such as taxi drivers, tour guides, or street vendors, should be avoided. Only use licensed taxis or

trustworthy transportation providers. Avoid walking in lonely or dark regions, and use secure spaces to examine your map and phone.

4. Be mindful of Costa Rica's natural risks and wildlife. Earthquakes, volcanic eruptions, landslides, floods, and storms are all common in the country. Follow the recommendations of the local authorities and keep an eye on the weather conditions before and during your travel. If you intend to climb, swim, surf, raft, zipline, or participate in any other outdoor activity, ensure that you have the necessary equipment, skills, and guides. Touching or feeding wild animals such as monkeys, sloths, snakes, spiders, scorpions, or bats is not permitted. If they feel threatened, they may transmit diseases or bite you.

5. In Costa Rica, dial 911 toll-free from any phone if you require medical treatment or emergency assistance. For road and air paramedic and ambulance assistance, call 128 or Tourism Care Medical Services at 2286-1818. Private doctors are mentioned in the Yellow Pages under

Médicos. Prepare to pay for any medical care either in advance or through your travel insurance. Methanol intoxication is widespread and can be lethal. Leave your drinks unattended and refuse drinks from strangers.

Money and Budget

The money exchange and budget for a vacation to Costa Rica in 2024 are determined by a variety of factors, including the exchange rate, inflation rate, season, and personal preferences.

To help you organize your vacation, here are general guidelines:

1. Currency: Costa Rica's currency is the colón (CRC), which is divisible into 100 céntimos. Banks, hotels, and authorized exchange offices can convert US dollars (USD) to colones. You can also use your credit or debit card at ATMs or stores that accept them. You may, however, be charged fees or charges for these transactions, so check with your bank before you go. As of October 8, 2023, 1 USD is worth 533.40 CRC.

However, due to market changes and economic situations, this rate may fluctuate over time. Various websites, such as Xe, Wise, WalletInvestor, and Trading Economics, provide current exchange rates. These sources also offer forecasts and historical data on the USD/CRC exchange rate.

2. Low budget: Expect to spend roughly $30-$40 each day if you want to travel as cheaply as possible. On this budget, you can stay in hostels or campgrounds, cook your meals or eat at local sodas (small restaurants), utilize public transportation or hitchhike, and participate in free or low-cost activities such as hiking, swimming, or animal watching. Some of the more popular attractions, such as national parks, ziplining, and surfing instruction, are prohibitively expensive.

3. Expensive: If you want to splurge on your trip and have a more comfortable and luxurious experience, you should budget $150-$200 per day. You can stay at good hotels or resorts, dine at fancy restaurants or worldwide chains, use private shuttles or taxis, and do whatever activity you choose on this budget. Tours and packages that include everything you need for your trip can also be booked.

4. Average budget: You can anticipate spending $60-$80 each day for a balanced trip that allows you to appreciate both the beauty and culture of Costa Rica without breaking the bank. On this budget, you can stay in mid-range hotels or guesthouses, dine at a variety of local and foreign restaurants, take shared shuttles or colectivos (shared taxis), and participate in certain paid activities such as visiting national parks, ziplining, and snorkeling. You can also hunt for offers or discounts online, or you can bargain with local providers.

Transportation and Getting Around

Here are some of the most popular modes of transportation in Costa Rica, along with their advantages and disadvantages.

1. Rent a car: Renting a car allows you to drive throughout Costa Rica at your own pace. You can get to regions that aren't accessible by public transit or shuttles, and you can stop whenever you want to enjoy the view or take a rest. Renting a car, on the other hand, can be costly, especially if you require a 4WD vehicle for rugged terrain or river crossings. You must additionally pay for mandatory liability insurance, gas, tolls, and parking. Driving in Costa Rica can be difficult because certain roads are in poor condition, are poorly marked, or are congested. You must also be aware of traffic laws, speed limits, and potential road hazards such as animals, pedestrians, and landslides. If you decide to rent a car, make sure to reserve ahead of time with a reliable firm, inspect the vehicle before driving, and navigate using a GPS or offline map app.

2. Shuttle Buses: Shuttle buses are comfortable vehicles that provide shared or individual transportation between famous Costa Rica sites. They are more convenient and speedier than public buses since they have scheduled schedules, online booking, and in many cases, door-to-door service. They are also less expensive than hiring a car or flying within the country. However, shuttle buses have restricted routes and availability, so you may be unable to reach some locations or go at the time of your choosing. You must also share the space with other passengers and adhere to the driver's schedule. If you prefer greater privacy or freedom, you can pay more for a private shuttle service, which allows you to create your schedule and travel at your own pace.

3. Domestic flight: Domestic flights are the quickest and easiest way to get around Costa Rica, especially if you are short on time or prefer not to drive great distances. Flying between major cities and tourist attractions takes less than an hour, saving you time and trouble. You may also get a birds-eye view of the country. Domestic flights, however, are the most expensive choice, and their availability or frequency may be limited depending on the season or weather conditions. You must also be aware of baggage weight limits and airport charges. If you want to fly within Costa Rica, make a reservation with one of the domestic airlines.

4. Public bus: Because they connect practically every town and village in Costa Rica, public buses are the cheapest and most authentic method to travel throughout the nation. On board, you can learn about the local culture and connect with pleasant passengers. Along the route, you can also enjoy the magnificent vistas. Public buses, on the other hand, are the slowest and least comfortable alternative because they make frequent stops, lack air conditioning and amenities, and might be crowded or delayed. You will also need to carefully arrange your trip around bus schedules and routes, which can change at any time. To pay for your tickets, you will also need cash in local currency (colones).

Chapter 2

Accommodation

Hostel

Hostels with a high budget

1. Selina Monteverde: This hostel is near the Monteverde Cloud Forest Reserve, which is one of the world's most biodiverse locations. From your accommodation, you may enjoy spectacular views of the mountains and forest, or participate in one of the hostel's various activities, such as yoga, hiking, zip-lining, or horseback riding. The hostel offers dorms, private rooms, a restaurant, a bar, a pool, and a co-working space. A dorm bed costs $25 on average, whereas a private room costs $75.

2. Witch's Rock Surf Camp: Located directly on Tamarindo Beach, one of Costa Rica's greatest surfing places, this hostel is ideal for surfers and beachgoers.

Learn to surf with skilled teachers, rent surfboards and equipment, or join a surf trip to local beaches. There's also a restaurant, a bar, a pool, and a spa in the hostel. A dorm bed costs around $30, while a private room costs over $70.

3. Selina Manuel Antonio: This hostel is close to the Manuel Antonio National Park, where you may view monkeys, sloths, and toucans. You can also spend your time relaxing on the magnificent beaches, snorkeling, kayaking, rafting, or exploring the nearby town of Quepos. The hostel offers a variety of lodging options, including tents and suites, as well as a restaurant, bar, pool, and co-working area. A dorm bed costs around $20, while a private room costs around $65.

Hostels on a Low Budget

1. Pagalu Hostel: This hostel is in Puerto Viejo de Talamanca, a vibrant Caribbean village. You may relax in town, visit the nearby Cahuita National Park, or rent a bike and ride along the coast. There are spacious dorm rooms with lockers and fans, a shared kitchen, a sitting space, and a garden at the hostel. A dorm bed costs an average of $10.

2. Nosara Beach Hostel: Nosara is a quiet town on the Pacific coast. You can go surfing at the famous Playa Guiones beach, take a yoga session, or view sea turtles at the neighboring Ostional Wildlife Refuge. Simple dorm rooms with fans and mosquito nets are available, as is a community kitchen, a sitting area with hammocks and reading, and complimentary bikes. A dorm bed costs around $12 on average.

3. Mitamon Hostel Airport: Located in Alajuela, near the San Jose International Airport, this hostel is a good option. It is ideal for those who need to catch an early flight or arrive late at night. The hostel includes air-conditioned dorm rooms with private toilets, as well as individual rooms with TVs and refrigerators. In addition, the hostel provides complimentary breakfast, airport shuttle service, Wi-Fi, and parking. A dorm bed costs an average of $15.

Hotel

Hotels on a High Budget

1. Four Seasons Resort Costa Rica at Peninsula Papagayo: This is Costa Rica's only Five-Star hotel, offering luxury amenities and suites on a hilltop. Yoga, chocolate making, volcanic mud treatments, and dining at a Latin-inspired fish house are among the activities available. In addition, the resort provides access to two beautiful beaches and a golf course. A one-night stay costs almost $1,000.

2. El Rodeo Estancia Boutique Hotel & Steakhouse: A wonderful hotel with a rustic design and a comfortable ambiance. You may unwind in the spacious apartments, which feature balconies, jacuzzis, and fireplaces, or you can enjoy the outdoor pool and garden. The hotel also includes a restaurant, which serves delectable meat dishes as well as regional delicacies. A one-night stay costs about $200.

3. Andaz Costa Rica Resort in Peninsula Papagayo:
A modern and trendy hotel that merges with the natural environment. From the open-air welcome area, you can take in views of Culebra Bay or explore the local forest paths and animals. There are four restaurants, three pools, a spa, and a kids club at the hotel. A one-night stay costs about $400.

Hotels in the Mid-Price Budget

1. Hotel Arco Iris: This is a welcoming and comfortable hotel in Tamarindo, a popular surfing and beach destination. Stay in one of the 13 rooms or suites, each with its own distinct design and decoration. In addition, the hotel offers a pool, a garden, and a restaurant serving Mediterranean cuisine. A one-night stay costs about $100.

2. Hotel Belmar: This is a lovely and eco-friendly hotel amid the cloud forest reserve of Monteverde. Each of the 25 rooms and suites has hardwood furniture and panoramic windows. A spa, a yoga studio, a farm-to-table restaurant, and a microbrewery are also available at the hotel. A one-night stay costs about $150.

3. Hotel Banana Azul: This beautiful and tropical hotel is located in the Caribbean beach resort of Puerto Viejo de Talamanca. Stay in one of the 22 apartments or villas, each with a hammock and a view of the garden. The hotel also offers a pool, a beach club, a bar, and a Caribbean-themed restaurant. A one-night stay costs about $80.

Hotels on the Low Budget

1. Selina La Fortuna: This is a pleasant and social hotel near the Arenal Volcano in La Fortuna. You can select between dorms and private rooms. There is also a pool, a coworking area, a cinema room, a yoga deck, and a restaurant serving local cuisine within the hotel. A one-night stay costs about $30.

2. Hotel La Amistad: A basic and decent hotel in San Jose, Costa Rica's capital city. Each of the 34 rooms has cable TV and complimentary Wi-Fi. The hotel also provides free breakfast, airport shuttle service, laundry service, and happy hour drinks. A one-night stay costs about $50.

3. Cabinas Jimenez: Located in Puerto Jimenez on the Osa Peninsula, this rustic and cheap hotel. You can stay in one of the 12 cabins or flats, which each include air conditioning and a kitchen. Guests can also borrow bikes, kayaks, and snorkeling equipment from the hotel. A one-night stay costs about $40.

Chapter 3

Costa Rica Cuisine

Here are some of the most popular and traditional foods to taste in Costa Rica, as well as their ingredients, preparation, and location.

1. Gallo Pinto: This is Costa Rica's national cuisine, and it can be found in practically any restaurant or household. It consists of white rice and black or red beans cooked with onion, sweet pepper, cilantro, and a sauce called Salsa Lizano. Gallo Pinto is typically served for breakfast, with eggs, cheese, tortillas, sour cream, and coffee on the side. However, it can also be served as a side dish or a main entrée for lunch or dinner. Gallo Pinto is popular throughout the United States, but particularly in the Central Valley.

2. Casado: Another popular lunch or dinner dish. A meal of rice, beans, salad, fried plantains, and your choice of meat (chicken, beef, pork, or fish). The name casado means "married" in Spanish, and it relates to the dish's mix of many components. Casado is a healthful and well-balanced meal that symbolizes the Costa Rican culture of blending many influences. Casado is available in the majority of restaurants and sodas (small eateries) around the country.

3. Ceviche: A tasty appetizer or snack made from fresh raw fish marinated in lime juice and seasoned with onion, cilantro, salt, and pepper. The lime juice "cooks" the fish and imparts a tart flavor to it. Ceviche is typically served cold, with crackers or tortilla chips on the side. To taste, you can also add tomato, avocado, or hot sauce. Ceviche is a popular meal on Costa Rica's Caribbean coast, where fresh seafood and tropical fruits may be found.

4. Olla de Carne: This substantial soup is ideal for chilly or wet weather. It contains meat chunks as well as potatoes, carrots, corn, cassava, plantains, and chayote. The soup is cooked for hours over low heat until the meat is tender and the stock is aromatic. Traditionally, Olla de Carne is served with rice and tortillas. It is a classic meal from the Central Valley, but it can be found in many places across the country.

5. Sopa de Mariscos: Similar to olla de carne, but made with fish and shellfish instead of beef. Coconut milk, garlic, onion, cilantro, and spices such as curry and ginger are used to make this soup. The end product is a substantial and delicious soup that is creamy and flavorful. Sopa de Mariscos is a Caribbean-style soup made with coconut milk.

6. Arroz with Camarones: This is a simple rice meal with shrimp that is wonderful. Rice is prepared with onion, garlic, sweet pepper, tomato sauce, chicken broth, and annatto (a natural coloring agent). Separately, the shrimp are cooked in butter, garlic, salt, and pepper. They're then combined with the rice and topped with cilantro. Arroz with Camarones is a popular meal on Costa Rica's two coasts, where shrimp are plentiful and fresh.

7. Arroz con Mariscos: Similar to arroz con camarones, but with a wider range of ingredients. Mussels, clams, squid, octopus, and fish are cooked with onion, garlic, sweet pepper, tomato sauce, chicken broth, and annatto, as well as mussels, garlic, sweet pepper, tomato sauce, chicken broth, and annatto.

Separately, the fish is cooked with butter, garlic, salt, and pepper before being combined with the rice. Arroz with Mariscos is a celebratory dish that is frequently served on special occasions or during the holidays. It's also popular in Costa Rica's two coasts, where the fish is numerous and varied.

8. Tamales: Are steamed corn-based dumplings wrapped in banana leaves. They're stuffed with a variety of meat, rice, vegetables, cheese, and seasonings. Tamales originated in Mexico, but have since been customized to the Costa Rican palate and ingredients. They are typically consumed over the holidays but can be found in some regions all year.

Tamales are a typical Costa Rican meal that honors the country's indigenous history.

Chapter 4

The Best of Costa Rica

Top 7 Attractions And Experiences

1. Manuel Antonio National Park: With good cause, this is one of Costa Rica's most popular and frequented national parks. It offers beautiful beaches, thick forests, a diverse wildlife population, and hiking routes. Monkeys, sloths, birds, reptiles, and other animals can all be seen in their natural habitat. Swim, surf, snorkel, or kayak in the pristine waters of the Pacific Ocean.

2. Arenal Volcano: This is one of the world's most active volcanoes and a breathtaking sight to behold. From numerous vantage points, you may observe its cone-shaped peak, or stroll around its base to discover lava flows and hot springs. There are also waterfalls, rivers, lakes, and forests in the nearby area. Arenal Volcano is also an excellent location for adventure activities including ziplining, rafting, horseback riding, and canopy tours.

3. Monteverde and the Cloud woodlands: These are high-altitude woodlands that are blanketed in mist and clouds, providing a magnificent environment. You can wander through the woods on hanging bridges or zipline above them. You can also learn about the varied flora and creatures that live in these forests, including orchids, hummingbirds, butterflies, and quetzals. Monteverde is also home to some of Costa Rica's greatest coffee, so don't pass up the opportunity to sample it at a local farm.

4. Tamarindo: This vibrant Pacific coast beach town attracts surfers, sunbathers, and partygoers. It boasts a long sandy beach with regular surf and quiet waters for swimming and snorkeling. Other water sports such as fishing, sailing, and stand-up paddle boarding are also available. Tamarindo offers a thriving nightlife scene that includes pubs, restaurants, and clubs for all interests and budgets.

5. Dominical: A more rustic and laidback beach village on the southern Pacific coast than Tamarindo. It boasts a beautiful beach with strong surf, as well as rocky coves and tide pools to explore. You can also go to local sites such as Marino Ballena National Park to witness whales and dolphins; Nauyaca Waterfalls to swim in natural pools; and Hacienda Baru Animals Refuge to trek and see animals.

6. Mal Pais and Santa Teresa: Mal Pais and Santa Teresa are two nearby beach villages on the Nicoya Peninsula that have grown popular with surfers, yogis, and celebrities. They boast stunning beaches with world-class surf and quiet coves and lagoons for swimming and snorkeling. In addition, these communities offer yoga lessons, spa treatments, and health vacations. Mal Pais and Santa Teresa have a bohemian and cosmopolitan vibe, with a diverse selection of restaurants, cafes, boutiques, and galleries.

7. Jaco: This is yet another lively beach town on the Pacific coast that provides guests with plenty of fun and entertainment. It features a lengthy beach with surfable waves and various water activities such as jet skiing and parasailing. You may also explore local sites such as Carara National Park, where you can witness crocodiles and scarlet macaws, or Tortuga Island, where you can enjoy a day trip with snorkeling and lunch. Jaco's nightlife is vibrant, including casinos, bars, discos, and live music.

Top 10 Wildlife Encounters

1. Sloths: These adorable, slow-moving mammals can be seen throughout Costa Rica, particularly in the rainforests. Most of the time, they hang upside down from trees, sleeping or eating leaves. They can be found in national parks such as Manuel Antonio, La Fortuna, and Monteverde, as well as wildlife refuges such as Sloth Sanctuary and Toucan Rescue Ranch.

2. Quetzals: With bright green and red feathers and long tail feathers, these birds are among the most beautiful and rare in the world. Many indigenous civilizations venerate them, and they serve as a symbol for Costa Rica. They live in high-altitude cloud forests and consume fruits and insects. The Monteverde Cloud Forest Reserve is the greatest site to see them, as they are most active during the mating season, which lasts from January to July.

3. Tapirs: These are large, odd-looking herbivores with a long snout for grabbing foliage and fruits. They are related to horses and rhinos but resemble pigs in appearance. Because they are nocturnal and fearful, they might be difficult to spot in the wild. Corcovado National Park is the ideal site to watch them, as they frequently visit the beach to cool off or drink water.

4. Sea Turtles: These elegant and ancient reptiles live in the sea but come to land to lay their eggs on sandy beaches. Costa Rica is home to various sea turtle species, including leatherbacks, green turtles, hawksbills, and olive ridges. Tortuguero National Park, where they nest year-round, and National Wildlife Refuge, where hundreds of olive ridleys arrive in mass nesting events known as arribadas, are the finest sites to watch them.

5. Monkeys: These intelligent and lively primates live in the jungle canopy. Costa Rica is home to four monkey species: howlers, capuchins, spider monkeys, and squirrel monkeys. They have various personalities and mannerisms, but they all make a lot of noise and havoc. You may view them in practically any national park or animal reserve in Costa Rica, although Manuel Antonio, Corcovado, and Cahuita are among the best.

6. Whales and dolphins: These beautiful and gregarious marine mammals can be seen in the warm waters along Costa Rica's Pacific and Caribbean shores. Whales and dolphins such as humpbacks, orcas, pilot whales, bottlenose dolphins, spinner dolphins, and spotted dolphins visit or reside in Costa Rica. Marino Ballena National Park, where humpbacks come to breed and calve from July to November and December to April, or Drake Bay, where you can watch whales and dolphins all year, are the greatest sites to see them.

7. Macaws: These huge, colorful parrots live in rainforests in pairs or flocks. They have strong beaks for cracking nuts and seeds and loud voices for communication. They are threatened by habitat destruction and illegal trade, but they can still be found in the wild in some regions. Carara National Park, where scarlet macaws soar over the river every day, and the Osa Peninsula, where scarlet macaws and large green macaws can be seen, are the greatest places to watch them.

8. Frogs: Are small and diverse amphibians that dwell in damp environments like ponds, streams, and leaf litter. Camouflage, poison glands, and sticky toes are just a few of their incredible adaptations. They're also extremely vocal at night, generating a symphony of sounds in the darkness. Costa Rica is home to approximately 200 frog species, some of which are extremely uncommon or endemic. The finest sites to see them are La Selva Biological Station, which has red-eyed tree frogs, poison dart frogs, glass frogs, and other frogs, and Monteverde Cloud Forest Reserve, which has resplendent tree frogs, rainforest rocket frogs, and harlequin toads.

9. Hummingbirds: This are small, fast-moving birds that feed on nectar from flowers. They can hover, fly backward, and change direction in a moment. They also have iridescent feathers that change color according to the angle of light. Costa Rica is home to approximately 50 hummingbird species, some of which are indigenous or endangered. Monteverde Cloud Forest Reserve, where you can witness violet saber wings, purple-throated mountain gems, or magenta-throated woodstars, and La Paz Waterfall Gardens, where you can see green-crowned brilliants, coppery-headed emeralds, or black-bellied hummingbirds, are the greatest sites to watch them.

10. Jaguars: These are the Americas' largest and most powerful cats, having a speckled coat that helps them blend in with the vegetation. They are apex predators, which means they have no natural predators and may hunt everything from deer and peccaries to caimans and turtles. Because they are solitary and elusive, they are extremely difficult to spot in the wild. Corcovado National Park is the ideal site to see them because it has a healthy population and they sometimes leave traces or scurry on the trails.

Top 10 Adventure Activities

1. Ziplining: Flying through the treetops on a zipline is an exciting and popular way to experience the Costa Rican rainforest. You may see stunning vistas of rich flora, waterfalls, volcanoes, and wildlife as you fly from platform to platform at breakneck speeds. There are several zipline tours offered throughout the country, but some of the best are in Monteverde Cloud Forest Reserve3, Arenal Volcano National Park, and Manuel Antonio National Park.

2. Whitewater Rafting: If you like fast-paced water sports, whitewater rafting in Costa Rica is for you. The country has some of the best rafting rivers in the world, with class I to V rapids depending on the season and location. You may see amazing vistas of the rainforest, mountains, and wildlife while paddling through the rapids with your guide and group. Among the most popular rafting destinations are the rivers Pacuare, Reventazon, Sarapiqui, and Savegre.

3. Surfing: Costa Rica is a surfer's dream, with more than 50 breakers on both the Pacific and Caribbean coasts. The waves are consistent and warm throughout the year, and there are locations for surfers of all levels, from beginners to pros. Surf schools, camps, and rentals are common in most seaside locations. Some of the world's top surfing beaches include Playa Grande, Tamarindo, Playa Negra, Dominical, Montezuma, and Santa Teresa.

4. Hiking: Costa Rica's natural beauty is rich and abundant, including volcanoes, jungles, cloud forests, beaches, and other attractions. Hiking is one of the best ways to discover and enjoy the beauty and biodiversity of the country. There are trails of different difficulty and length, ranging from casual hikes to demanding adventures. The hiking routes in Corcovado, Rincón de la Vieja, Chirripo, and Tenorio Volcano National Parks are among the best in the world.

5. Snorkeling and Diving: Costa Rica boasts a stunning underwater environment teeming with colorful coral reefs, tropical fish, turtles, rays, sharks, dolphins, and whales, among other things. Snorkeling and diving are fantastic ways to discover and enjoy the country's marine life and scenery. Most coastal towns offer snorkeling and diving excursions as well as equipment rentals. Some of the best snorkeling and diving locations are Cahuita National Park, Isla del Coco National Park, Isla Tortuga, and Cano Island Biological Reserve.

6. Wildlife Viewing: Costa Rica is one of the world's most biodiverse countries, with over 500,000 animal and plant species. Wildlife viewing is one of the major draws and joys of visiting Costa Rica. Monkeys, sloths, toucans, macaws, hummingbirds, frogs, butterflies, crocodiles, jaguars, tapirs, and other animals can all be seen in their natural habitats. You can also go on guided tours or visit wildlife sanctuaries and rescue facilities to learn more about the animals and conservation efforts. Among the best places to see wildlife are Tortuguero National Park, Monteverde Cloud Forest Reserve 3, Manuel Antonio National Park, and La Selva Biological Station.

7. Hot Springs: Costa Rica has several geothermal hot springs as a result of volcanic activity. Hot springs are naturally formed pools of mineral-rich water heated by the earth's core. They are relaxing, tranquil, and good for the body and mind. Hot springs can be found in a wide range of settings, from natural rivers to luxurious resorts. Some of the best places to go for hot springs include Arenal Volcano National Park, Rincon de la Vieja National Park, Orosi Valley, and San Gerardo de Dota.

8. Kayaking: Kayaking is an exciting and adventurous way to explore Costa Rica's waterways and coasts. You can kayak over mangroves, rivers, lakes, lagoons, estuaries, or oceans, depending on your preferences and skill level. You might see birds, monkeys, turtles, dolphins, or crocodiles along the way. Kayaking tours and rentals are offered at the majority of water-based destinations. Some of the best places to kayak in Costa Rica are Tortuguero National Park, Lake Arenal, Golfo Dulce, and Tamarindo Estuary.

9. Horseback Riding: A traditional and romantic way to learn about Costa Rica's culture and landscape. You can ride through the countryside, villages, forests, beaches, or mountains, depending on your location and preferences. You can also learn about the history and culture of the locals by engaging with them. The majority of rural areas provide horseback riding tours and rentals. Some of the best places to go horseback riding are in La Fortuna, Monteverde, Nosara, and Turrialba.

10. Bungee Jumping: Consider bungee jumping in Costa Rica for the ultimate adrenaline sensation. Bungee jumping is an extreme sport in which you leap from a high platform while being held by an elastic cord around your ankles. You may experience a free fall and a rebound as you drop toward the ground and then bounce back up. Bungee jump locations include bridges, cranes, and towers. Among the best places to go bungee jumping are Monteverde Extremo Park, Tropical Bungee, and Gravity Falls Waterfall Jumping.

Top 10 Cultural Events And Festivals

Costa Rica is a country that enjoys celebrating its traditions, history, and identity throughout the year through various events and festivals. Whether you enjoy music, art, religion, or sports, Costa Rica has a festival for you.

Here are some of the most popular and intriguing ones to attend during your next visit to this tropical paradise.

1. Imagine Festival

Every February, the Envision Festival, a four-day celebration of art, music, yoga, and spirituality, takes place in the coastal forest of Uvita. This festival attracts visitors from all over the world who wish to immerse themselves in the local culture and nature. You can attend live performances by local and international artists, participate in workshops and classes on a variety of topics, browse the organic market and food booths, or simply unwind in the healing zone. Envision Festival is a community of like-minded people who share a vision of harmony and sustainability.

2. Carnival Lmon

Every October, the Caribbean province of Limón hosts the Lmon Carnival. With colorful parades, live music, dancing, cuisine, and drinks, this carnival celebrates the Afro-Caribbean heritage and culture of the region. You can watch the carnival queen be chosen, attend street parties and performances, or try Limón's delectable cuisine. The Lemon Carnival is a dynamic and exciting celebration that promotes Costa Rica's diversity and joy.

3. Festival de Palmares

Palmares Festival is a two-week festival held in the town of Palmares in January. It is considered the country's largest cowboy event, including horse parades, carnival rides, concerts, bullfights, and plenty of alcohol. across a million tourists come from all across the country and beyond to enjoy the festive mood and entertainment. The Palmares Festival is a lively and thrilling event that highlights Costa Rica's rural and traditional side.

4. Diablitos Fiesta

Fiesta de los Diablitos (Festival of the Little Devils) is a three-day festival held in the indigenous village of Boruca in December or January. It is a symbolic recreation of the Boruca people's resistance against Spanish conquerors. Masked dancers dressed as diablitos (small devils) representing the Boruca culture and a toro (bull) representing the Spanish invaders take part in the festivities. The diablitos use sticks and firecrackers to pursue and defeat the toro on the last day. Fiesta de los Diablitos is a one-of-a-kind and fascinating event dedicated to preserving and honoring Costa Rica's indigenous culture.

5. International Arts Festival

The International Arts Festival (FIA) is a biennial event held in San José in March or April. It is one of Costa Rica's major cultural events, showcasing local and international performers from a variety of genres including theater, dance, music, cinema, literature, visual arts, and more. The festival features both free and paid concerts in various locations throughout the city, as well as workshops, exhibitions, and street acts. The International Arts Festival is a fantastic opportunity to explore and appreciate Costa Rica's and other countries' artistic ability and diversity.

6. Los Angeles Virgin Day

The Virgin of Los Angeles Day (Da de la Virgen de los Angeles) is a national holiday celebrated on August 2nd each year. It honors La Negrita (The Black Madonna), Costa Rica's patron saint, who is said to have appeared to a peasant child in Cartago in 1635. The celebration includes a pilgrimage (Romera) from San José to Cartago when hundreds of devout walk to the Basilica of Our Lady of Los Angeles. There, people pray, give offerings, and implore La Negrita for miracles. The

Virgin of Los Angeles Day is a religious and cultural celebration that symbolizes Costa Ricans' faith and devotion.

7. Independence Day

Independence Day (Da de la Independencia) is a national holiday celebrated on September 15th every year. It commemorates Costa Rica's 1821 independence from Spain. Throughout the country, patriotic parades, rituals, speeches, and fireworks are held. The torch run (torches), in which students carry torches from Guatemala to Costa Rica to signify the arrival of the independence news, is one of the most iconic customs. Another custom is to sing the national song and raise the flag at 6 p.m., followed by a lantern parade (faroles) in which children hold lanterns of all forms and colors. Independence Day is a proud and festive celebration of Costa Rica's history and identity.

8. Carnival / Dia de los Muertos

Carnival / Dia de la Raza (Day of the Race) is an October 12th national holiday. It honors Costa Rica's diversity and multiculturalism, as well as Christopher Columbus' 1492 discovery of America. The celebration includes parades, dances, costumes, and music representing Costa Rica's various ethnic groups and cultures. The most notable carnival takes place in Puerto Limón, which has a significant Afro-Caribbean flavor. Carnival / Dia de la Raza is a bright and joyful event that celebrates Costa Rica's diversity and richness.

9. Virgin of the Sea Fiesta

Fiesta de la Virgen del Mar (Fiesta de la Virgen del Mar) is a religious and nautical celebration held in Puntarenas in July. It is named for the Virgin of Mount Carmel, who is said to have saved the lives of a group of fishermen during a storm in 1926. A procession of boats decked with flowers and flags transports a statue of the Virgin from Puntarenas to Playa Naranjo as part of the celebration. There is music, food, and prayer. The Fiesta of the Virgin of the Sea is a maritime and spiritual celebration honoring Puntarenas' patron saint.

10. Ocaso Underground Music Festival

Ocaso Underground Music event is a five-day music event held in Tamarindo in January. It is one of Costa Rica's most prominent electronic music festivals, with local and international DJs and producers performing underground genres such as techno, house, deep house, and others. The event hosts parties in a variety of settings, including beaches, jungles, pools, and clubs, where you can dance, mingle, and soak up the tropical atmosphere. Ocaso Underground Music Festival is a fantastic venue for music fans looking to have a good time and discover new sounds.

Nightlife And Entertainment

1. Beach and Pool Parties: Bask in the tropical ambiance of Costa Rica's beautiful beaches, where you may party all night with music, cocktails, and cuisine. Tamarindo, Jaco, Puerto Viejo, and Manuel Antonio are just a few of the top beach towns for nightlife. You can also participate in entertaining and festive beach and pool tours that take you to various locations by bus or boat.

2. Pubs and Clubs: Enjoy the urban nightlife of San Jose, Costa Rica's capital city, where there are pubs and clubs to suit every taste and inclination. Irish pubs, sports bars, wine bars, cigar bars, jazz clubs, salsa clubs, reggae bars, and more venues can be found. San Jose's most popular nightlife districts include La California, Barrio Escalante, San Pedro, and Escazu.

3. Art and Culture: Explore Costa Rica's creative and cultural side, where you'll find places showcasing local talent and originality. There are museums, art galleries, theaters, cinemas, and cultural centers where you can see shows, events, performances, and exhibitions. Cafes, pubs, and restaurants host live concerts, comedy evenings, poetry readings, open mic nights, and other events.

4. Casinos and Gambling: Try your luck in one of Costa Rica's many casinos. Hotels and resorts across the country have bingo halls, slot machines, table games, poker rooms, and other amenities. San Jose is home to several of the city's most prominent casinos, including the Fiesta Casino, the Hotel Del Rey Casino, and the Casino Club Colonial. Casinos can also be found in Tamarindo, Jaco, Liberia, and Quepos.

Chapter 5

Destination Guides

San José and Central Valley

San José is known as the "Vibrant Capital."
With a population of over one million, San José is Costa Rica's largest and most cosmopolitan city. It is a vibrant and colorful city with museums, theaters, parks, markets, restaurants, bars, and nightclubs.

1. The National Museum, which depicts Costa Rica's history and culture from pre-Columbian origins to the present. It is housed in a historic military fortification, and bullet holes from the 1948 Civil War may still be seen.

2. The Gold Museum, which houses a significant collection of gold artifacts from diverse indigenous

tribes. It also features currency, numismatics, and banking exhibitions.

3. The Jade Museum, which houses the greatest jade collection in the United States. Ceramics, fabrics, and stone sculptures are also on display.

4. The National Theater, is a magnificent neoclassical structure that stages opera, ballet, music, and theater acts. It is recognized as a national icon of artistic brilliance in Costa Rica.

5. The Central Market, is a bustling and colorful marketplace where you can buy fresh fruits and vegetables, meat and cheese, coffee, souvenirs, and other items. It's also a fantastic spot to enjoy traditional Mexican foods like Gallo pinto (rice and beans), casado (mixed plate), and chorizo (fried pork with beans and salsa).

6. The La Sabana Metropolitan Park, is a sprawling green park with sports fields, playgrounds, lakes, and

pathways. It also serves as the primary location for soccer events and concerts.

A Natural Wonderland is the Central Valley

The Central Valley is both an urban and natural playground. The neighboring mountains and countryside offer several sights and activities. As an example,

1. You can explore one of three nearby volcano national parks: Iraz, Poás, or Barva. The craters, lakes, fumaroles, and vents of these volcanoes provide breathtaking views. Trails lead to cloud forests, waterfalls, rivers, and wildlife.

2. Visit the Orosi Valley, which is recognized for its scenic beauty, colonial history, and coffee culture. It is home to one of Costa Rica's oldest churches, the Basilica of Our Lady of the Angels, which was built in 1639. It also boasts multiple coffee plantations, which produce some of the world's greatest coffee.

3. The Zoo Ave Wildlife Rescue Center, a haven for injured or orphaned animals, is open for visits. More

than 100 bird, mammal, reptile, and amphibian species can be seen. You can also find out more about their conservation efforts and adopt an animal.

4. The Adventure Park is a fun and exciting location for adrenaline junkies. Ziplining, bungee jumping, rappelling, canopy tours, paintballing, and other activities are available.

Costa Rica's Central Valley has something to offer everyone. It combines urban convenience with rural charm, modern development with historical legacies, and cultural diversity with national identity. It's a place where you may get a taste of Costa Rica's essence: pura vida (pure living).

Caribbean Coast

Costa Rica's Caribbean Coast is a place of breathtaking natural beauty, diverse cultural heritage, and plentiful wildlife. It has a wide range of sights and activities for visitors who wish to see a different side of Costa Rica away from the more popular locations.

The following are the of the Caribbean Coast's highlights:

1. Tortuguero National Park: This park is one of the world's most important green sea turtle hatching grounds. Take a boat excursion through the park's network of canals and lagoons to see the varied plants and creatures that live in this wetland ecosystem. You can also go to Tortuguero to learn about the local culture and history.

2. Cahuita National Park: This park preserves a coral reef, which is home to hundreds of fish species, as well as dolphins, sharks, rays, and sea turtles. Snorkel or scuba dive in the clean waters, or trek along the coastal trail, which winds between tropical trees and white-sand beaches. You can also go to Cahuita to experience Afro-Caribbean cuisine and music.

3. Puerto Viejo de Talamanca: Popular with hikers, surfers, and partygoers. It features a vibrant nightlife with bars, restaurants, and clubs playing reggae, salsa, and calypso music. You can also go surfing, swimming, or relaxing on the surrounding beaches of Playa Negra, Playa Cocles, and Punta Uva.

4. Manzanillo Wildlife Refuge: This refuge is a haven for nature enthusiasts, allowing them to experience the unspoiled beauty of the rainforest and the sea. Hiking routes lead to waterfalls, rivers, and vistas, and kayaking along the shore allows you to see dolphins, manatees, and crocodiles. You can also visit the village of Manzanillo to learn about the Bribr people's unique culture.

Northern Lowlands

Costa Rica's Northern Lowlands are a diversified range of scenery, fauna, and attractions. This place has something for everyone, whether you want adventure, nature, or culture.

The Arenal Volcano, which was active until 2010 and still offers breathtaking views of its cone and lava fields, is one of the Northern Lowlands' main draws. You may relax by the volcano's hot springs, waterfalls, and hiking trails, or you can attempt some adrenaline-pumping sports like zip-lining, rafting, or canyoning. Arenal is also a gateway to other attractions in the area, such as the Cao Negro Wetlands, a seasonal lake and marsh that is home to numerous birds and animals, and the Venado Caves, a limestone cavern system with stalactites, stalagmites, and bats.

Tortuguero National Park, a lonely and rugged location only accessible by boat or plane, is another highlight of the Northern Lowlands. From July to October, Tortuguero is famous for its turtle nesting beaches, where you may see sea turtles laying eggs or hatching. The park also contains a network of canals and lagoons that are home to a plethora of animals, including monkeys, crocodiles, sloths, and toucans. These rivers can be explored by boat, kayak, or canoe, or by hiking the rainforest paths.

Visit some of the small towns and villages in the Northern Lowlands, where agriculture and conservation coexist. You can learn about the local culture and history, try native cuisine and goods such as pineapple, banana, and sugarcane, or engage in community-based tourism projects that benefit the environment and the people. Puerto Viejo de Sarapiqu, a gateway to the middle of nowhere; Ecocentro Danaus, an animal rescue center and volunteer project; Heliconia Island, a botanical garden with exotic flowers; and Proyecto Asis, a wildlife refuge and Spanish school, are just a few of the sites you may explore.

Guanacaste and Northwest Pacific Coast

Guanacaste and the Northwest Pacific Coast of Costa Rica are destinations that cater to travelers of all interests and preferences. This region has something for everyone, whether they want adventure, nature, culture, or relaxation.

Here are the recommendations for visitors to Guanacaste and the Northwest Pacific Coast of Costa Rica:

1. Rincon de la Vieja National Park: One of the region's most diverse and exciting places to explore. There's an active volcano, geothermal activity, waterfalls, hot springs, mud baths, and wildlife to enjoy. Hiking through the tropical dry forest, swimming under cascades, soaking in mineral pools, and exhilarating adventures like ziplining, tubing, horseback riding, and rappelling are all available. Las Pailas and Santa Maria are the park's main gates. Las Pailas is more convenient for Liberia and has more facilities and trails, but Santa Maria is more distant and rustic. The park is open from 8 a.m. to 3 p.m., with a $15 admission cost per person.

2. Beaches: The region is home to some of Costa Rica's most stunning and diverse beaches. There are white sand beaches, black sand beaches, rocky beaches, and shell beaches, each with its personality and beauty. The following are some of the most well-known beaches:

- **Tamarindo Beach:** This busy surf town attracts a lot of visitors because of its waves, nightlife, and gastronomy. Surfing lessons, kayak rentals, catamaran cruises, and market shopping are all options. Tamarindo also features a variety of lodging alternatives, ranging from low-cost hostels to opulent resorts.

- **Playa Conchal:** One of the most beautiful beaches in the area, with turquoise waves and a crushed seashell beachfront. Snorkel among the colorful fish, relax on the sand, or have a picnic under the trees. The Westin Golf Resort & Spa, a premium all-inclusive resort with golf, tennis, spa, and dining, is also located on Playa Conchal.

- **Playa Hermosa:** This is a tranquil and laid-back beach ideal for sunbathing and relaxing. Swimming and kayaking are great in the quiet and clean lake. Along the seaside in Playa

Hermosa, you may also enjoy a cool drink or a delicious dinner.

- **Nosara:** This is a peaceful seaside town that attracts visitors looking for a more quiet and holistic experience. Yoga retreats, wellness centers, and organic eateries are well-known in Nosara. The beach is also a wonderful place for beginners and advanced surfers.

- **Santa Teresa:** This is a bohemian coastal town popular with surfers, yoga practitioners, and nature lovers. There is a thriving surf culture in Santa Teresa, with numerous surf shops, schools, and camps. The beach is also surrounded by a thick jungle, where monkeys, birds, and butterflies can be seen. There are also several restaurants and pubs in Santa Teresa that include live music and entertainment.

- **Montezuma:** A delightful coastal hamlet that embodies bohemian beach living. Montezuma offers a relaxed atmosphere, an artistic culture, and breathtaking waterfalls hidden in the neighboring woods. Hiking to the waterfalls, swimming in natural pools, or taking a canopy tour over the forest are all options.

3. Culture: The region is also culturally and historically rich. You can learn about the indigenous Chorotega people who lived in the area before the arrival of the Spanish. **You can also see colonial towns and churches from the 18th century. Cultural attractions include:**

- **Liberia:** The capital of Guanacaste province and the region's principal entry point. Liberia's colonial architecture reflects the country's past as a cattle ranching community. You may visit the Museo de Guanacaste, which exhibits the province's history and culture; the Iglesia de la Agonia, one of Costa Rica's oldest churches; or the Parque Central, a vibrant center where you can mingle with locals.

- **Santa Cruz:** This is one of Guanacaste's most traditional communities and the birthplace of Costa Rican folklore. Throughout the year, Santa Cruz hosts a variety of cultural events such as patron saint celebrations, rodeos (bull riding), topes (horse parades), marimba concerts (traditional music), and bailes tipicos (folk dances). You can also go to the Museo de Cultura Guanacasteca (Guanacaste Culture Museum), which shows objects and costumes from local customs.

- **Nicoya:** This is one of Costa Rica's oldest towns and the hub of the Nicoya Peninsula. Nicoya has a rich history and culture that has been affected by indigenous, Spanish, and African influences. The Iglesia de San Blas, Costa Rica's oldest church, can be visited, as can the Museo Etnografico de Nicoya (Ethnographic Museum of Nicoya), which displays the region's pre-Columbian and colonial history, and the Mercado Municipal (Municipal Market), where you can buy fresh produce, handicrafts, and souvenirs.

Nicoya Peninsula

The Nicoya Peninsula is an area in Costa Rica with a distinct charm and way of life. It is one of the world's five Blue Zones, where people live longer and healthier lives than the norm because of their lifestyle, nutrition, and surroundings. The Nicoya Peninsula has beautiful beaches, lush woods, unique fauna, and a welcoming culture.

The best way to get there

The Nicoya Peninsula is separated from the mainland by the Tempisque River and the Gulf of Nicoya. You can fly, drive, bus, or ferry there. Flying from San Jose to one of the local airports in Tambor, Nosara, or Samara is the quickest method. You can alternatively drive to Puntarenas and then take a ferry to Paquera or Naranjo. You can then hire a car or take another bus to your final destination. Keep in mind that some roads are dirt and can be difficult to navigate, especially during the wet season.

Places to stay

The Nicoya Peninsula offers a wide range of hotel options to suit every budget and taste. Luxury hotels, eco-lodges, beachside bungalows, hostels, and vacation rentals are all available.

The following are a few of the most popular places to stay:

1. The Retreat Nicoya Peninsula: A holiday rental property that provides seclusion and tranquillity in your private sanctuary.

2. Hotel Punta Islita: A five-star resort with a golf course, a spa, an infinity pool, and breathtaking Pacific Ocean views.

3. Harmony Hotel: In Nosara, there is a boutique hotel that mixes sustainability and wellness.

4. Florblanca Resort: In Santa Teresa is a romantic getaway with spacious villas, a yoga studio, a surf school, and a gourmet restaurant.

5. Ylang Ylang Beach Resort: In Montezuma, a tropical haven with modest cabins, a yoga deck, a spa, and a beachfront restaurant.

What should you do?

Nature lovers, adventure seekers, and wellness aficionados will find heaven on the Nicoya Peninsula. **There are numerous activities and attractions available, including:**

1. Surfing: With consistent waves and warm water all year round, the Nicoya Peninsula is one of the best spots in the world to surf. From beginner-friendly beaches like Samara and Nosara to demanding waves like Malpais and Santa Teresa, there are surf opportunities for everyone.

2. Yoga: The Nicoya Peninsula is a popular destination for yoga enthusiasts, with numerous studios and classes accessible throughout the region. Yoga styles range from hatha to vinyasa to aerial yoga. Yoga retreats and programs that mix yoga with other activities like meditation, hiking, or horseback riding are also available.

3. Hiking: There are many natural reserves and parks on the Nicoya Peninsula where you may hike and enjoy the area's rich flora and fauna. The Cabo Blanco Nature Reserve, Costa Rica's first protected area, has stunning white-sand beaches and numerous wildlife. Hiking to the Montezuma Waterfall, a beautiful cascade that cascades into a natural pool surrounded by thick flora is another option.

4. Zip-lining: For a thrill and excitement, try zip-lining through the jungle canopy. Zip-line tours are available at a variety of spots throughout the peninsula, including Montezuma, Malpais, and Samara. You will see unique wildlife such as monkeys, sloths, and toucans as well as stunning vistas of the countryside.

5. Kayaking: Another way to appreciate the Nicoya Peninsula's beauty is to go kayaking on its tranquil waters. Kayak along the Gulf of Nicoya to witness dolphins, whales, turtles, and mangroves. Kayak on the Rio Nosara to see crocodiles, birds, and bats.

When should I leave?

The optimum time to visit the Nicoya Peninsula is determined by your objectives. From December to April, the dry season delivers sunny days and clear skies. This is also the peak season for tourists and surfing, so rates will be higher and there will be more people. From May to November, the rainy season offers colder temperatures and the occasional shower. Because it is also the off-season for tourism and surfing, expect reduced pricing and fewer crowds. However, due to flooding or mudslides, certain roads may be impassable.

Chapter 6

Practical Information

Emergency Contacts

However, it, like any other country, has its own set of risks and crises that visitors should be aware of and prepared for. In the event of an emergency, various services and organizations can assist and support both visitors and locals.

The 911 number, which is the national emergency system and works 24 hours a day, seven days a week, is one of the most significant emergency contacts in Costa Rica. You can contact the police, fire department, ambulance, Red Cross, and other emergency services by dialing 911. The operators can communicate in both English and Spanish, and they can also connect you with other agencies or institutions if necessary.

The US Embassy in San José, which provides consular services to US citizens and nationals in the country, is another point of contact in case of an emergency. The embassy can aid with passport replacement, medical situations, legal assistance, arrests, fatalities, and other disasters. The embassy's phone number is +506-2519-2000, and it is located at Calle 98 Va 104, Pavas. For US citizens, the embassy also maintains an after-hours emergency number at +506-2220-3127.

If you are going with a tour operator or a travel agency, keep their emergency contact information ready as well. They can assist you with any concerns or issues about your vacation arrangements, including transportation, lodging, activities, and reservations. They can also give you local advice and information on how to handle any problems or issues that may arise during your vacation.

In addition to these emergency contacts, there are a few other numbers and resources you can utilize if you are in Costa Rica and there is an emergency. **As an example,**

1. If you require medical assistance or guidance, contact the Costa Rican Social Security System (CCSS) at +506-2539-0000, which operates public hospitals and clinics around the country.

2. If you need to report a crime or a security incident, contact Costa Rica's principal law enforcement body, the Judicial Investigation body (OIJ), at +506-800-8000-645.

3. If you need to contact your airline or check the status of your flight, call the Juan Santamaria International Airport (SJO), which is located near San José, at +506-2437-2400.

Local And Costum Etiquette

Costa Ricans, often known as Ticos, are noted for their kindness, hospitality, and regard for others. Visitors should be aware of basic local customs and etiquette to avoid misunderstandings and have a pleasant stay. **Here are a few of the most significant:**

1. Greetings: Depending on the level of familiarity and gender, Costa Ricans greet each other with a handshake, an embrace, or a kiss on the cheek. Men normally shake hands, however, ladies may hug or kiss each other on the right cheek. A handshake is customary among strangers or acquaintances when greeting someone of the opposite sex, whereas a hug or kiss may be suitable among friends or relatives. Depending on the time of day, say "Buenos das," "Buenas tardes," or "Buenas noches."

2. Titles: When addressing people, Costa Ricans are formal and respectful, particularly seniors, professionals, and authorities. They employ titles like "Seor" (Mr.), "Seora" (Mrs.), "Seorita" (Miss), "Don" (Sir), or "Doa" (Madame) followed by the person's first or last name. "Don José" or "Doa Mara" are two examples. They also use academic or professional titles like "Doctor", "Ingeniero" (Engineer), "Profesor" (Teacher), or "Abogado" (Lawyer) followed by their surname. "Doctor Pérez" or "Profesora González" are examples. It is considered impolite to address someone solely by their first name unless they specifically invite you to do so.

4. Personal space: Costa Ricans are warm and friendly individuals who prefer to keep close physical touch throughout chats. They may brush against your arm, shoulder, or back, or stand closer to you than usual. This is not a violation of your personal space, but a gesture of camaraderie and trust. Touching someone's head, hair, or face, on the other hand, may be interpreted as disrespectful or personal. You should also avoid looking at strangers' personal space.

5. Dining: Costa Ricans like dining with family and friends, and they are generous and welcoming hosts. If you are asked to have a meal at someone's house, you should attend on time or slightly late, but not too early. You should also bring a small gift to demonstrate your appreciation, such as flowers, chocolates, wine, or liquor. Wait for your host to encourage you to sit down and begin eating, and then follow their lead on whether to eat with your hands or with utensils. You should taste everything and commend both the meal and the chef. You should not leave any food on your plate because it may be considered wasteful or insulting. Offer to help with the dishes or clean up after the dinner.

6. Tipping: Most restaurant, hotel, and other service bills in Costa Rica include a 10% service charge. Tipping is not required or expected, but it is welcomed if you receive great service or wish to express your appreciation. Depending on your level of satisfaction, you can tip 5% to 10% of the bill. You can also tip taxi drivers, tour guides, porters, and other service workers.

Costa Rica has a tropical climate that varies depending on height and region. As a result, dress appropriately for the weather and the occasion. For everyday activities such as shopping, sightseeing, or visiting friends, Costa Ricans dress casually but neatly. They dress comfortably in shorts, t-shirts, sandals, or sneakers. They do, however, dress more professionally for jobs, school, church, and social functions. They dress up in suits, dresses, skirts, blouses, and heels. They also avoid wearing outfits that are too revealing or provocative, as this may attract unwelcome attention or insult local sensitivities.

10. Pura Vida: Costa Rica's motto is "pura vida," which translates to "pure life." It symbolizes the country's upbeat outlook on life, as well as its love of nature, serenity, and happiness. Costa Ricans use this phrase to welcome one another, express gratitude, say goodbye, or praise something pleasant. As an example,

- How are you today? Viva la Vida!
- Thank you for your assistance. Viva la Vida!
- We'll talk later. Viva la Vida!
- This beach is gorgeous. Viva la Vida!

This remark can also be used when talking with locals to demonstrate your respect for their culture and the pleasure of their nation.

These are some of the most important parts of Costa Rican etiquette to be aware of before visiting this amazing country. You can prevent cultural misunderstandings and make a good impression on your hosts and friends if you follow these guidelines. You will also have the opportunity to experience the genuine meaning of "pura vida" and have an unforgettable and delightful time in Costa Rica.

Communication

Costa Rica's primary language is Spanish, but there are five indigenous languages as well as English.

1. Spanish: This is Costa Rica's official language and the most widely spoken. It differs from Spanish spoken in other countries in that it includes some unique words and idioms. "Hola, cómo está usted?" means "Hello, how are you?"

2. Maléku: One of Costa Rica's indigenous languages, spoken by the Maléku people of the north-eastern Alajuela Province. It is a threatened language, with only about 600 speakers remaining. A communication sentence in Maléku is: "Naná kái kái kái kái kái kái kái kái kái kái kái kái", which means "I am very happy".

3. Cabécar: The Cabécar people of the Talamanca mountain range and the southern Pacific region speak this indigenous Costa Rican language. It is a Chibchan language linked to other Central and South American languages. A communication statement in Cabécar is: "Sëkë sëkë sëkë sëkë sëkë sëkë sëkë sëkë sëkë sëkë sëkë sëkë", which means "Thank you very much" .

4. Bribri: This is Costa Rica's third indigenous language, spoken by the Bribri people of the country's Atlantic slope, which includes Limón Province and the Talamanca mountain region. It, too, is a Chibchan language with a complicated grammatical structure. A communication statement in Bribri is: "Sulú sulú sulú sulú sulú sulú sulú sulú sulú sulú sulú sulú", which means "Good morning"

5. Guam: The Guam people speak this fourth indigenous language of Costa Rica, which is spoken in diverse indigenous regions to the southeast of Puntarenas Province, bordering Panama. It is also a Chibchan language with some dialects. A communication sentence in Guaymí is: "Nö nö nö nö nö nö nö nö nö nö nö ", which means"Hello " .

6. Buglere: This is Costa Rica's fifth indigenous language, spoken by the Buglere people, who share the same territory as Guam. It is closely linked to Guam and is considered a dialect of Guam by some linguists. A communication sentence in Buglere is: "Bügü bügü bügü bügü bügü bügü bügü bügü bügü bügü bügü", which means "Goodbye".

7. English: This is the most widely used foreign language in Costa Rica, particularly in cities and tourism areas. Many Costa Ricans learn English in school or through private lessons, and some have lived or studied in other countries. English is also the primary commercial and commerce language of Costa Rica. In English, a communication sentence is "How are you?"

Shopping and Market

Various things, ranging from handicrafts and souvenirs to apparel and technology, can be found in various locations throughout the country.

Here are Costa Rica's greatest shopping areas:

1. Mercado Central: San Jose, Costa Rica's capital city, has a central market. It's a lively market with many little kiosks and tight lanes selling everything from clothes, souvenirs, and groceries to fresh flowers, local food, and cigars. You may also sample some amazing coffee at Cafe Central or taste some delicious local food at the soda cafes.

2. Mercado Nacional de Artesania: In San Jose, you may buy handcrafted items manufactured by local craftsmen at the national craft market. Paintings, sculptures, ceramics, fabrics, beads, jewelry, wood and leather products, and other items can be found. The rates are modest, and you may bargain with pleasant vendors who know English.

3. Avenida Escazu: Located in the wealthy Escazu district, this is one of Costa Rica's most elegant shopping complexes. It boasts a modern design and a laid-back attitude, as well as a variety of stores, restaurants, and a theater. There are both worldwide brands and local boutiques selling clothing, accessories, home decor, books, and other items.

4. La Feria Legendaria de Playa Chiquita: This is a beachside market on Costa Rica's Caribbean coast in Playa Chiquita. Every Saturday from 9 a.m. to 2 p.m., it features a wide range of products from local vendors and artisans. Organic food, natural cosmetics, handmade jewelry, art, apparel, crystals, and other items are available. The market also has live music and yoga lessons.

5. Galeria Namu: Located in San Jose, this art gallery and gift shop specializes in indigenous and folk art from Costa Rica and other Central American countries. There are masks, baskets, pottery, fabrics, paintings, carvings, and other items available. Prices are reasonable, and the quality is excellent. In addition, the business promotes fair trade and social projects that benefit artists and their communities.

Packing Essentials

Packing for Costa Rica, on the other hand, can be difficult due to the country's diverse weather and activities

Here are packing tips for Costa Rica visitors:

1. Luggage: Depending on your travel style and itinerary, a backpack, a suitcase, or both may be appropriate. A backpack is more useful for hiking, camping, or traveling frequently, whereas a suitcase allows you to arrange and retrieve your items more easily. If you bring both, make sure they are light and durable because you may have to carry them on difficult roads or uneven terrain. You should also bring a compact day bag with you for your daily necessities like water, sunscreen, a camera, and snacks.

2. Clothing/Apparel: Costa Rica has a tropical climate, but temperature and rainfall vary by location and elevation. The weather may be hot and humid by the shore, cool and dry in the highlands, or rainy and windy in the rainforest. As a result, it is best to pack layers that can be adjusted based on the conditions. Pack lightweight and quick-drying apparel, such as shorts, t-shirts, tank tops, dresses, and skirts. Cotton and denim should be avoided as they take longer to dry and can mold.

- Long pants and long-sleeved shirts, preferably made of breathable, moisture-wicking materials. These are useful for sun, pest, and plant protection, as well as cooler nights or higher altitudes.

- A raincoat or poncho, especially if traveling during the rainy season (May-November). For further protection, carry an umbrella or a hat.

- A sweater or fleece jacket for cool nights or mornings. If you are visiting regions like Monteverde or Poas Volcano, where the temperature can fall below 10°C (50°F), you may also require a warmer jacket.

- Beach or pool attire and a cover-up. If you intend to surf or snorkel, you should carry a rash guard or a wetsuit.

- Socks and undergarments. Pack plenty for your trip, or bring clothes that can be washed and dried easily. For colder climates, you may want to bring warm underwear or wool socks.
- Sunglasses, a hat or cap, a scarf or bandana, and a belt are examples of accessories. These can be used to complement your clothing while also protecting you from the sun or dust.

3. Footwear: Hiking, zip line, rafting, horseback riding, and other outdoor activities are available in Costa Rica. As a result, you must bring comfortable and durable footwear that can withstand a variety of terrains and climates. Hiking shoes or boots, ideally waterproof and with high traction, should be packed. These are required for visiting national parks, volcanoes, waterfalls, and other natural wonders.

- Sandals or flip-flops with straps or buckles are preferred. These are ideal for going for a walk on the beach, relaxing at a hotel, or taking a shower.

- Sneakers or other casual footwear. These are useful for getting around town, visiting museums or markets, or using the bus or taxi.

4. Toiletries and accessories: Although Costa Rica has many modern conveniences and services, it is nevertheless recommended that you bring some personal goods to make your trip more comfortable and pleasurable. You should bring the following accessories and toiletries: - Sunscreen with SPF 30+. Because Costa Rica lies near the equator, the sun is quite hot and can cause sunburns or skin damage. Throughout the day, liberally and regularly apply sunscreen.

5. Repellent against mosquitos: There are numerous mosquitoes and other insects in Costa Rica that can bite you and spread diseases like malaria or dengue fever. Use a repellent containing the active component DEET or picaridin.

6. A first-aid kit: Although Costa Rica has excellent healthcare facilities and pharmacies, it is always a good idea to have some basic supplies on hand in case of minor accidents or illnesses. Bandages, antiseptic wipes, pain relievers, anti-diarrhea medications, antihistamines, and any prescription medication you require should all be included in your kit.

7. A bottle of water and purification tablets: Although most of Costa Rica has potable water, it is always best to be safe than sorry. Bring a reusable water bottle as well as water purification tablets or drops in case you are in a remote location or have a sensitive stomach.

8. A headlight or a flashlight: Power outages are common in Costa Rica, especially during the rainy season. In the event of an emergency, a flashlight or headlamp can help you see in the dark and attract attention.

9. A camera with a charger: Costa Rica has beautiful scenery, wildlife, and culture. You'll want to document your experiences and share them with friends and family.

Bring a camera that meets your requirements and tastes, as well as a charger and spare batteries or memory cards.

- An adapter as well as a converter. Costa Rica has the same voltage and plug type as the United States, so you may not require an adaptor or converter if you are traveling from that country. If you are traveling from another nation, you may need to bring one or both of these items.

10. Passport (original and copies): To enter Costa Rica, you must have a valid passport, as well as a return ticket or proof of onward travel. Check that your passport is valid for at least six months and has enough blank pages for stamps. You should also include duplicates of your passport and other critical documents, such as your driver's license, credit cards, and insurance cards, just in case you misplace or lose them.

Chapter 7

Travel Itinerary Planner

There are numerous ways to organize a trip to Costa Rica based on your tastes, money, and time constraints. Here are itineraries for various lengths of travel:

A Day

If you just have one day to see Costa Rica, you should focus on one region or activity that piques your interest. For example, you may go to San Jose, the capital city, and see the National Theater, the Gold Museum, and the Central Market. Alternatively, you may visit one of the many national parks and reserves in Costa Rica, such as Poas Volcano, Manuel Antonio, or Monteverde, and appreciate the nature and wildlife. Alternatively, you might spend the day relaxing on one of the Pacific or Caribbean coast's stunning beaches, such as Tamarindo, Jaco, or Puerto Viejo.

1 week

A week in Costa Rica allows you to experience more of the country's diversity and beauty.

A week's agenda could include:

Day 1: Arrive in San Jose and start exploring.

Day 2: Visit Poas Volcano National Park for a day trip to witness the magnificent crater and lake. You may also observe butterflies, hummingbirds, and orchids at the adjacent La Paz Waterfall Gardens.

Day 3: Visit Arenal Volcano National Park in La Fortuna. Hiking around the volcano, viewing the lava flows, and relaxing in the hot springs are all options.

Day 4: Go zip-lining, rafting, or canyoning in La Fortuna. You may also glimpse the turquoise waters of the Rio Celeste Waterfall, which is nearby.

Day 5: Visit the Monteverde Cloud Forest Reserve. You can walk across the hanging bridges, observe quetzals and other species, and learn about conservation initiatives.

Day 6: Visit Manuel Antonio National Park. There are monkeys, sloths, and other wildlife to see, as well as beautiful beaches.

Day 7: Depart from San Jose.

2 Weeks

You can see more of Costa Rica's attractions and hidden treasures if you have two weeks to travel.

A two-week itinerary could include:

Day 1: Arrive in San Jose and start exploring.

Day 2: Visit the Irazu Volcano National Park and see Costa Rica's highest volcano. You can also go to the nearby city of Cartago to admire its colonial architecture and church.

Day 3: Visit Tortuguero National Park. You may take a canal boat excursion to see turtles, crocodiles, and birds.

Day 4: Visit Puerto Viejo and soak in the Caribbean atmosphere. You can witness coral reefs and wildlife at Cahuita National Park.

Day 5: Visit the islands and beaches of Bocas del Toro, Panama. The clean seas are ideal for snorkeling, surfing, and kayaking.

Day 6: Visit Turrialba Volcano National Park. You can also go rafting on the Pacuare River or mountain biking on the routes.

Day 7: Visit Arenal Volcano National Park in La Fortuna. Hiking around the volcano, viewing the lava flows, and relaxing in the hot springs are all options.

Day 8: Go zip-lining, rafting, or canyoning in La Fortuna. You may also glimpse the turquoise waters of the Rio Celeste Waterfall, which is nearby.

Day 9: Visit the Monteverde Cloud Forest Reserve. You can walk across the hanging bridges, observe quetzals and other species, and learn about conservation initiatives.

Day 10: Visit Santa Teresa and soak up the surf culture. You can surf, relax, or practice yoga on its beaches.

Day 11: Visit Isla Tortuga for a day trip to witness its white sand beach and crystal clear ocean. This island paradise offers snorkeling, swimming, and sunbathing opportunities.

Day 12: Visit Jaco and take in the nightlife. You may also observe crocodiles, macaws, and other animals at the Carara National Park.

Day 13: Visit Manuel Antonio National Park. There are monkeys, sloths, and other wildlife to see, as well as beautiful beaches.

Day 14: Depart from San Jose.

Conclusion

The Costa Rica Travel Guide was created as a labor of love, with the utmost care and attention to present you, the tourist, with a thorough and insightful reference for visiting this beautiful nation. I've tried to capture the essence of Costa Rica in these pages, with its natural beauty, colorful culture, and spirit of adventure.

As a travel writer, my goal has always been to take readers to Costa Rica's beautiful jungles, clean beaches, and towering volcanoes, which make the country a true paradise. I've shown you the beauties of its different landscapes, which range from foggy cloud forests teaming with rare species to vivid coral reefs bursting with marine life. I've taken you on a journey through history, revealing the rich history and traditions that create this country's identity.

However, the goal of this guide is to inspire you to start on your own adventure and make lifelong memories. From navigating transportation options to finding the ideal lodging, I've offered practical suggestions and guidance to guarantee a seamless and pleasurable journey. I've encouraged you to embrace sustainable tourism practices so that we may all work together to preserve Costa Rica's natural wonders for future generations.

I hope you experienced the kindness and hospitality of the Costa Rican people, who embody the Pura Vida lifestyle, during your trip. This is a worldview that emphasizes joy, gratitude, and a strong connection to nature. It is a call to slow down, relish every moment, and embrace the little joys that surround us.

As you put this book down and prepare to embark on your journey, I'd like to leave you with one final thought: Costa Rica is more than a destination; it's an experience that will touch your heart and soul. It is a destination where you may go on exhilarating adventures, immerse yourself in colorful local culture, or simply relax in nature's embrace. It's a spot that will make an indelible impression on your soul.

So, dear traveler, pack your bags, open your heart to the delights that await, and allow Costa Rica to guide you on a once-in-a-lifetime adventure. May your travels be filled with breathtaking scenery, new friendships, and a deep appreciation for the splendor of this magnificent country. Have fun!

Printed in Great Britain
by Amazon

35045716R00059